Life Lessons from the Book of Ruth:

A Pageantry of Destiny

by

Garnet Nowell

Inspiration Flows

Printed in the United States of America

First Printing: 2021

Published by Inspiration Flows

Broken Arrow, OK 74012

www.inspirationflows.com

Cover design: Copyright © 2021 CANVA

Contents

Introduction

I love the Book of Ruth, not because she found a husband; good for her. This book, like Esther, speaks to me. This story of one of purpose and how God orchestrates the infinite moments and seasons of our lives. Ruth's story is one of those stories in which we see Ruth unknowingly pursue her destiny, which was planned for her before she was born. Follow me on this incredible journey of discovery through the Book of Ruth, and you will see that destiny simply means keeping God's appointments. Though God's presence seems to be absent in most of the story, He makes Himself known as we study the pageantry of this encouraging and inspiring drama.

We learn from life lessons every day, such as teaching your children not to run into the street and not touch hot objects. The Book of Ruth, though only four short chapters, is full of life lessons for us to follow. I promise you; you will not think of Ruth in the same way after reading this book.

What's in a Name?

Naomi (Delight or Pleasant One), her husband, Elimelech (God is my King), and sons, Mahlon (Infirmity) and Chilion (Consumption), moved to Moab during the times of the Judges because there was a famine in the land. The first life lesson is about names. I was taught early in my walk with the Lord to be careful about what you name your children. There was a young man who was in school with my daughter; his name caused a few problems. Unfortunately, he had the same name as a kid in the horror movie, The Omen. His name was Damien, and the other kids teased this kid mercilessly. So much so that his adoptive parents had his name legally changed.

Names describe the purpose and character of a person. In scripture, names carry both power and authority. We were commanded never to use His name in vain and to honor His name. The names of God describe His character, nature, and attributes. Some of God's names include:

- El Shaddai: God Almighty, All-Sufficient One (God who nourishes, satisfies, protects, and blesses) – Genesis 17:1, Exodus 6:3, Psalm 91:1,2

- El Elyon: Most High God (Extremely-Exalted, Sovereign God) – Genesis 14:19, Isaiah 14:13-14, Daniel 7:18

- El Echad: The One God (There is only one true God) – Malachi 2:10

- El Emet: The God of Truth (Faithful and Reliable) – Psalm 31:5

- El Chaiyim: The Living God (God of my life) – Psalm 42:8

- El Gibbor: The Strong and Mighty God – Isaiah 9:6

- El Roi: The God Who Sees Me – Genesis 16:13

Through His names, God reveals His power, strength, purpose, and love for His people. These are only a few of His names that show His divine character.

Elimelech gave his boys terrible names. Why do you suppose Naomi and Elimelech gave their sons such

dreadful names? Could it be possible that hearing themselves called Infirmity and Consumption caused their premature deaths? Mark 11:23-24 informs us that we will have what we say. Imagine Mahlon and Chilion constantly hearing their parents (and everyone else) say to them, you are sick, you are failing, and you are wasting away. Where is the blessing in that? Life and death are genuinely in the power of the tongue (Proverbs 8:21).

Proverbs 22:1 tells us, "A good name is more desirable than great riches; to be esteemed is better than silver or gold." Elimelech, Naomi's husband, was a man who held God in high esteem. He was a member of the tribe of Judah, a native of Bethlehem Judea, a man of wealth, and probably the head of a family or clan. His name is found only once in the Bible (Ruth 1:2). According to the Abarim Biblical Hebrew Dictionary, "Chilion is not very cheerful. It's spelled the same way as and pronounced slightly different from the noun כליון (*killayon*), meaning failing or annihilation, derived from the verb כלה (*kala*), meaning to come to an end." No, not very cheerful at all. Chilion marries Orpah, a Moabite woman while dwelling in Moab. He died, leaving his wife a widow and his mother,

Naomi, who had already lost her husband, grieving again when her son died.

Naomi's other son, Mahon (sickly), marries Ruth. Mahlon is a derivative of the verb חלה (*hala*), meaning weak, sick, or wounded. The name literally means 'man of weakness' (*Abarim*).

As parents, we must protect our children, even before their birth. Consider the seven times God named children before they were born (or possibly conceived):

1. **Isaac** (Genesis 17:19) – "But God replied, No— Sarah, your wife, will give birth to a son for you. You will name him Isaac, and I will confirm my covenant with him and his descendants as an everlasting covenant."

2. **Ishmael** (Genesis 16:11) – "And the angel also said, you are now pregnant and will give birth to a son. You are to name him Ishmael (which means 'God hears'), for the Lord has heard your cry of distress."

3. **Solomon** (1 Chronicles 22:9) – "But you will have a son who will be a man of peace. I will give him peace with his enemies in all the surrounding lands.

His name will be Solomon, and I will give peace and quiet to Israel during his reign."

4. **Josiah** (1 Kings 13:2) – "Then at the Lord's command, he shouted, "O altar, altar! This is what the Lord says: A child named Josiah will be born into the dynasty of David."

5. **Cyrus** (Isaiah 45:1-7) – "This is what the Lord says to Cyrus, his anointed one whose right hand he will empower. Before him, mighty kings will be paralyzed with fear. Their fortress gates will be opened, never to shut again. This is what the Lord says I will go before you, Cyrus, and level the mountains. I will smash down gates of bronze and cut through bars of iron. And I will give you treasures hidden in the darkness— secret riches. I will do this so you may know that I am the Lord, the God of Israel, the one who calls you by name. And why have I called you for this work? Why did I call you by name when you did not know me? It is for the sake of Jacob, my servant, Israel, my chosen one. I am the Lord; there is no other God. I have equipped you for battle, though you

don't even know me, so all the world from east to west will know there is no other God. I am the Lord, and there is no other. I create the light and make the darkness. I send good times and bad times. I, the Lord, am the one who does these things."

6. **John the Baptist** (Luke 1:13) - "But the angel said, Don't be afraid, Zechariah! God has heard your prayer. Your wife, Elizabeth, will give you a son, and you are to name him John."

7. **Jesus** (Luke 1:30-31- NLT) – "Don't be afraid, Mary, the angel told her, for you have found favor with God! You will conceive and give birth to a son, and you will name him Jesus."

God had a plan for these seven, whom He named before their birth. Their names were a part of their planned destiny. So what's in a name? A name signifies your destiny and tells the world the story of who you were born to be. God changed Abram's name (*Noble Father*) to Abraham (*Father of Many*) in Genesis 17:4-6; thus, Abraham became the progenitor of a great nation. If you

are a believer in the Lord Jesus Christ, you are a spiritual descendant of Abraham.

Elimelech's choice in naming his sons could have possibly doomed them from the start. Their names signify that they would be weak and sickly and wasting away from a young age, leaving their family to combat a massive amount of grief.

The life lesson to be learned is to be very careful when choosing names for your children and speaking over other areas of your life. Your tongue is a creative force. Stop speaking doubt and unbelief and start calling those things in your life, which appear to be dead as though they were very much alive and striving (Romans 4:17).

I'm Hungry; Are We There Yet?

Your blessing is tied to a place (*there*), not to your stomach. God often gives us directions to our next assignment, and we can either listen and obey or choose to go our own way. When Elimelech decided to leave Bethlehem (place of bread) and move to Moab (place of the curse), did he leave his *there*? Even though Elimelech's original plan was to sojourn (temporarily) in Moab, he was there for a considerable amount of time. When God's people choose to leave the place of blessing because of the hardships they face and choose instead of the comforts of the world, they may discover they have traded their family's spiritual lives for worldly pleasures.

If we look closely at Naomi, who returned to Bethlehem, we will not see that same person who went to Moab many years before (Ruth 1:19). Bethlehem was the place of the family's continued blessing. Some have speculated that the deaths of Elimelech, Mahlon, and Chilion are a direct result of Elimelech's move to Moab. Did he choose to forsake God during a time when "men were doing what they thought to be right in their own eyes"

(Judges 21:25)? Judges reveal a time when God's people (for 300 years) are stuck in a vicious and destructive cycle of:

- *Apostasy*: The people turned away from God. A new generation arose who did not know the Lord nor the works He had done; thus, they did evil in the sight of the Lord.
- *Judgment and Repentance*: God's anger burned hot against Israel. He turned them over to their enemies.
- *Mercy and Deliverance*: When they repented, God raised up judges to deliver them out of the hands of their enemies.
- *Back into Apostasy*: The cycle repeated itself again and again (*Sin-Judgement-Repentance-Deliverance*).

Elimelech found himself and his family in this type of world. These were the times when he was contemplating whether he should go or whether to stay. In Ruth, we see a man making this decision based on what he thought was *right in his own eyes*, not based on God's Word.

Elimelech left God's land, God's people, and went to a place where the people worshipped false gods. The people of Moab worshiped Chemosh and Baal Peor with obscene rites and sometimes with human sacrifices. Should Elimelech have stayed in Bethlehem instead of moving to the cursed land of Moab? I, too, question this move to a cursed city away from the blessed house of bread (Bethlehem). Here is what we know about Moab:

- Moab means the *seed of the father or the desirable land.*
- Name of the eldest son of Lot (Genesis 19:37). Lot, Abraham's nephew, resided in Sodom when God destroyed the city. His wife died while fleeing the destruction of Sodom (pillar of salt) because of her disobedience.
- Lot fathered a child with his two daughters. This incestuous union produced two nations, the Ammonites and the Moabites (my pastor called them the '*ite*' boys).

- The name denotes the people of Moab (Numbers 22:3-14).
- David conquered Moab (2 Samuel 8:2)
- Children of Israel camped in Moab before entering the land of Canaan (Numbers 22:1)
- Moses died there (Deuteronomy 34:5).

Other notable things we know about Moab include:

1. Moabite women lead the men of Israel into sin during the Exodus (Numbers 25:1-2
2. Leads King Solomon into sin (1 Kings 11)
3. Offspring of the unions between Israel and Moab are barred (up to ten generations) from entering the assembly of Yahweh (Deuteronomy 23:3)
4. The Moabite king, Balak, hires Balaam to curse the Israelites (Numbers 22-24)
5. Israel and Moab share a great-grandfather in Terah, Abraham's father (Genesis 11:27)
6. Prophetic Destruction - Amos (Amos 2:1-2), Isaiah (Isaiah 15-16, Isaiah 25:10-12), Jeremiah (Jeremiah 48), and Ezekiel (Ezekiel 25:8-11) all prophesy the destruction of Moab.

7. In Isaiah 15, Moab's doom is announced, and then the fulfillment of the prophecy takes place within three years (Isaiah 16:13). King Nebuchadnezzar had the pleasure of completing the final desolation of Moab in 582 B.C.

We currently have an abundance of information concerning Moab that we can look at to decide if it is an excellent place to raise a family. However, Elimelech had to make a decision that he felt was best for his family at the time. Did he make the right decision?

According to Ruth 1:21, Elimelech was not poor and suffering hunger when he left Bethlehem. No, he was *full*. Those who were wealthy were sought out in those *lean seasons* to aid the poor. Perhaps he was afraid he would lose his wealth if he stayed in Bethlehem during the famine. Ruth 2:1 dispels that story. Boaz was a wealthy man before, during, and after the famine. Boaz stayed in Bethlehem during the famine and remained *full*.

The life lesson is to pray before we make decisions based on fear. He feared that the place where he was currently living would cause him to lose his wealth or die of starvation. Therefore, Elimelech decided he would

maintain his status by going *there,* not staying *here.* He did

not realize is that his blessings, and the blessings of his

family, are dependent on a place. Geography matters to

God. Did you know one of the names of God is Jehovah

Shammah :יְהוָה שָׁמָּה [The Lord (Self-existing One) Who is

There]? *There* signifies God's desire to be always present

with us. He never leaves us nor forsakes us, even in times

of famine.

Remember the story of Elijah? God sent Elijah to

the brook and told him to stay there. "Now Elijah the

Tishbite, who was of the settlers of Gilead, said to Ahab,

"As the LORD, the God of Israel lives, before whom I stand,

there shall be neither dew nor rain these years, except by

my word." And the word of the LORD came to him,

saying, "Go from here and turn eastward and hide yourself

by the brook Cherith, which is east of the Jordan

[River]. You shall drink from the brook, and I have

commanded the ravens to sustain you there [with

food]." So he went and did in accordance with the word of

the LORD; he went and lived by the brook Cherith, which is

east of the Jordan. And the ravens brought him bread and

meat in the morning, and bread and meat in the evening;

and he would drink from the brook (1 Kings 17:1-6). If Elijah had decided to go to another location, we would be reading a different version of this story. If God told the birds to feed Elijah, He could provide for Elimelech. I am sure He would have no problem feeding Elimelech and his family in the midst of famine. God *commanded* the ravens, which means to command, appoint, ordain (of a divine act). He caused them to do something entirely different from their normal behavior. Ravens are known to be scavengers and hoard food, not share it with other species. The ravens were appointed to bring him meat and did so.

In his commentary on 1 Kings 17, Matthew Henry states, "Let those who have but from hand to mouth, learn to live upon Providence and trust it for the bread of the day, in the day. God could have sent angels to minister to him, but he chose to show that he can serve his own purposes by the meanest creatures, as effectually as by the mightiest. Elijah seems to have continued thus above a year. The natural supply of water, which came by common providence, failed; but the miraculous supply of food, made sure to him by promise, failed not." What was that promise? God had promised him food provided by ravens,

and God kept his promise. In his haste to leave Bethlehem (***there***), Elimelech did not wait for God to use ravens or anything else to sustain him in the famine. He did not trust providence.

Another example of being at the right place is in 2 Kings 5. Naaman, commander of the Syrian army, wanted to be healed of his leprosy and was told by Elisha to wash seven times in the Jordan River; however, Naaman, in his pride, refused. He became angry and went away in a rage (2 Kings 5:11-12). He thought very highly of himself and thought he knew better than the prophet. Thus, without being obedient to the words of the prophet, Naaman would not have been healed (2 Kings 5: 1-14).

Always follow God's leading. Sometimes it may seem like an evil plan, but God already knows what is ahead of you and what is behind you. He can provide for you in famine and feast. Believe me, I know. I have been in both feast and famine, and God has always come through.

Go Where God Tells You to Go

When Naomi's husband and sons died, leaving her
alone with her two daughters-in-law, Ruth and Orpah,
Naomi decided to leave Moab and return to her people in
Judah. She advised the two girls to return to their people.
These two girls were of Moabite origins and grew up
worshipping the pagan gods of the Moabites. They married
Naomi's sons Mahlon and Chilion (aka *Infirmity* and
Consumption). Their husbands died, and Orpah left to
return to her people; however, Ruth chose not to go. Ruth
begged Naomi to let her continue on the journey with her.
Ruth made a conscious choice to follow Naomi, not only
pledging allegiance to Naomi but Naomi's God.

Ruth recognized God's leading, and she followed
her heart toward more abundant rewards (Ruth 1:16-17).
Ruth pledged loyalty, not only to Naomi but to Yahweh.
Brady (2013) maintains that this text represents Ruth's
conversion. Naomi asks her to turn back on three separate
occasions, and Ruth firmly tells Naomi that she will not
turn back but will follow her wherever she goes (Ruth 1:8-
15). After the fourth time, Naomi relents and allows Ruth

to go with her back to Bethlehem. Ruth's reply (Ruth 1:16-17), Don't force me to leave you; don't make me go home. Where you go, I go; and where you live, I'll live. Your people are my people; your God is my God; where you die, I'll die, and that's where I'll be buried, so help me GOD—not even death itself is going to come between us!

Here is the Jewish Targum's interpretation of how this conversation transpired,

> "Ruth said, Do not urge me to leave you, to go back from after you, for *I desire to be a proselyte.* Naomi then responds with the beginning of the proselyte's examination:
>
> *Naomi said, We are commanded to keep Sabbaths and holy days such that we may not walk more than two thousand cubits.*
>
> *Ruth said,* Wherever you go, I will go. *Naomi said, We are commanded not to lodge with Gentiles.*
>
> *Ruth said,* Where you lodge, I will lodge. *Naomi said, We are commanded to keep six hundred and thirteen commandments.*
>
> *Ruth said, What* your people *keep? I will keep as if they were* my people *from before this.*

Naomi said, We are commanded not to worship foreign gods.

Ruth said, Your god is my god.

Naomi said, We have four death penalties for the guilty: stoning with stones, burning with fire, execution by the sword, and hanging on a tree.

Ruth said, How you die, I shall die.

Naomi said, We have a cemetery.

Ruth said, And there I will be buried.

And do not say anymore. May the Lord do thus to me and more *against me* if even death shall separate me from you" (p. 137).

Ruth's last statement seals the deal. She decided to go where Naomi's God (now her God) told her to go. Being obedient to what she felt in her heart was from God, she procured a future for Naomi and herself. Remember this life lesson; obedience is better than sacrifice (1 Samuel 15:22).

Honor Your Mentors

The concept of mentoring is emphasized in both the Old and New Testaments of the Bible. Deuteronomy 6:4-9 is a guide for mentoring those in your family. First of all, the command is to love the Lord with all your heart and all your soul; then to teach the Word to your children.

In the New Testament, Jesus taught us how to mentor from a community perspective. Matthew 22:36-40 admonishes us once again to love the Lord with all your heart, soul, and mind; then, to love your neighbors as yourselves. This commandment was meant to establish relationships through which we can share the Word of God. In Romans 15:14 (NLT), Paul encourages us with these words: "I am fully convinced, my dear brothers and sisters, that you are full of goodness. You know these things so well you can teach each other all about them." Jesus, in Matthew 28, commands the disciples to go out and teach others to obey everything He had taught them.

We have been given many mentors to help us on this journey we call life. Sometimes we think we know more than our mentors; however, we need to follow the

instruction given in Proverbs 1:5, "A wise man will hear and increase in learning, and a man of understanding will attain wise counsel..." (NKJV). When God wants to bless you, He finds the right person to place in your life. I remember as a young Christian, I had a couple of mentors, including my pastors. God put a fired-up, anointed woman of God in my life to direct me during those early years. I will never forget the advice she gave me. She was like a second mom to my daughter and a big sister to me. We often talk, pray for each other, and share Godly wisdom.

As Christians, we judge others too quickly based on appearance or social status. We question God with silly questions about *why* this person is trying to gain access to me or give me instruction. Often, we make decisions based on incorrect assumptions, which can derail God's plan for our lives. When this happens, we want to blame someone else (or God), when in reality, we made the mistake of not trusting our mentors' advice.

Naomi was Ruth's mentor, and Ruth allowed Naomi to guide her decisions. In Ruth 2:22, Naomi exclaimed, "Do as he said, my daughter. Stay with his

young women right through the whole harvest. You might be harassed in other fields, but you'll be safe with him."

She further mentored Ruth on how to let Boaz know she was interested in a relationship. In Ruth 3:3-4, Naomi tells her, "Now do as I tell you—take a bath and put on perfume and dress in your nicest clothes. Then go to the threshing floor, but don't let Boaz see you until he has finished eating and drinking. Be sure to notice where he lies down; then go and uncover his feet and lie down there. He will tell you what to do."

This arrangement may seem strange to us; however, both Ruth and Naomi were pious and virtuous women, and Boaz (kinsman) had shown himself to be honorable. However, we cannot overlook the fact that Naomi's advice may have caused Boaz (if not for his own piety and what he knew about Ruth) to see Ruth as a loose woman and quite unfit to be his wife.

As we study the scriptures, we see God's plan in bringing these two together. In Ruth 2:12, Boaz blesses Ruth by stating, "May the Lord, the God of Israel, under whose *wings* you have come to take refuge, reward you fully for what you have done." When Ruth speaks to Boaz

on the threshing floor, she says to him, I am Ruth, your servant, "spread your *cloak* (or wing of your garment) over me, for you are a family redeemer." She is acknowledging that she is willing to find refuge both under the Lord's wings and under Boaz's as well. Wings (כָּנָף) kanaph, signifies an edge or extremity; specifically, (of a bird or army) a wing, (of a garment or bed-clothing) a flap. The same word used in Ruth 2:12 for *a wing* is used in Ruth 3:9 for *cloak* (or covering). God spoke to Ruth and Boaz, letting them know there was a divine connection, and they both would be covered by the God who cares for us enough to carry us on the wings of eagles, so we are forever loved and forever protected.

Naomi continues to mentor her by instructing her, "Just be patient, my daughter, until we hear what happens. The man won't rest until he has settled things today" (Ruth 3:18). Ruth did not argue with Naomi or offer any criticism concerning her instructions. Ruth 3:5 states, "I will do everything you say, Ruth replied."

The master of the field, Boaz, became her mentor as well. Thinking of her safety, Boaz advised Ruth to stay close to his workers and not wander into another field

(Ruth 2:8-10). Boaz also became her spiritual mentor by pronouncing a spiritual blessing upon her, "May the Lord repay you for what you have done. May you be richly rewarded by the Lord, the God of Israel, under whose wings you have come to take refuge"- Ruth 2:12 (NIV).

There are times when we pray for someone to be blessed; God will use us as the grantor of that blessing. Boaz became a blessing to Ruth in many ways, including providing for her immediate needs of food and safety and later as her husband.

What should you look for in a good mentor? Here are some other Biblical examples:

* Jethro mentored Moses (Exodus 1:13-26)

* Elijah mentored Elisha (2 Kings 2)

* Mordecai mentored Esther (Esther 2:20)

* Paul mentored Timothy (2 Timothy 1)

* Jesus mentored the disciples (Matthew 24, Luke 9)

Effective mentors give God credit for who we become; we teach others to be amazed by Christ in us, the only hope of glory. As mentors, we must be humble, and

we must have a personal relationship with Jesus Christ. Furthermore, mentors must live a life of thanksgiving to God. It's more about what God has done in our lives. Remember this life lesson because Godly mentors are a blessing; honor them. As Paul said, "And you should imitate me, just as I imitate Christ" (1 Corinthians 11:1).

Be Ready to Change with the Seasons

Ruth started working the fields at the beginning of the barley harvest and worked through the wheat harvest. Ruth stayed and only worked in the fields of Boaz through a change in seasons.

Ruth could have gone to work in other fields; however, she would have missed the blessings God had prepared for her (Ruth 2:23). Barley is the first grain harvested during the spring (around Passover); it is a hardy grain that can withstand harsh conditions, unlike wheat. Passover symbolizes Christ's giving of Himself as our Redeemer, and Boaz became Ruth's redeemer (Ruth 3:8-13). As her redeemer, Boaz was responsible for preserving the life, property, honor, and family name of his close relative (Naomi). He was presumably the *Goel* (redeemer or next-of-kin).

Ruth withstood many harsh conditions while in Moab and on the way to Bethlehem; however, she was willing to stay strong during the change in seasons, thus receiving the blessing of Pentecost (Exodus 23:24-33).

Typically, the Book of Ruth is read on Pentecost (Shavuot). According to the *Israel Institute of Biblical Studies*, there are various reasons for reading Ruth on Pentecost (Shavuot).

The main reason for this schedule of events is due to the agricultural calendar. The three festivals found in (Exodus 23:14) demonstrate crucial events in the annual agrarian cycle beginning with Passover (April), Pentecost ends the wheat harvest, and then begins the fruit harvest (June), with Tabernacles finishing the fruit harvest (October).

The book of Ruth provides an excellent picture of ancient Israelite agricultural practices, including reaping, gleaning, threshing, and winnowing. The story of Ruth takes place around the harvest calendar. When Naomi and Ruth return from Moab to Judah, the text says: "They arrived in Bethlehem at the beginning of the barley harvest" (1:22).

Additionally, Ruth is read on Shavuot to preserve the genealogy of the characters. Ruth and Boaz marry and have a son. The Word of God tells us, "They named him Obed; he became the father of Jesse, the father of David"

(Ruth 4:17). Ruth becomes the great-grandmother of King David. The connection with Shavuot is that King David was both born and died on Shavuot,
therefore, it is reasonable to read about David's genealogical line on his birthday (Lipnick, 2015, para. 4). A third reason to read Ruth on Shavuot concerns Ruth's courageous decision to join the nation of Israel. Ruth 1:16-17 records Ruth's words to Naomi, "Do not *urge* me to leave you or to turn back from following you! Where you go, I will go; where you lodge, I will lodge; your people shall be my people, and your God my God. Where you die, I will die—there will I be buried. May the LORD do thus and so to me, and more as well, if even death parts me from you!"

The use of the word *urge* (to aggressively press up against someone, even afflicting them physically) demonstrates that Ruth was strongly advising Naomi that she was going with her to Bethlehem, and there was nothing Naomi or anyone else could say or do to stop her. She endured the passage of each season, and as the seasons changed, her life changed for the better. Even though her father-in-law, Elimelech, journeyed from a place of

blessing to a place of curse, Ruth, in her wisdom, reversed that curse. She went from a cursed place to a place of great blessing. This life lesson offers encouragement to those going through difficult seasons. Remember, seasons are change agents. I urge you to continue to trust God in each new season and watch Him do exceedingly and abundantly above what you asked or expected (Ephesians 3:20).

Never Let Grief Overwhelm You

There is nothing wrong with grieving; however, you should never become bitter at the loss of something (or someone) you loved. The period of mourning in the Old Testament varied, usually depending on the importance of the deceased individual. Naomi lost her husband and two sons within a short period (Ruth 1:1-5). Her loss grieved her, but she was also bitter. Ruth also lost her husband, her brother-in-law, and her father-in-law (Ruth 1:5).

Both of these women suffered a significant loss; however, they reacted differently to those losses. Naomi became bitter because of what she had lost (Ruth 1:13-20). I call this Naomi's whining (*murmuring, complaining, groaning*) passage. Every word out of her mouth was negative, and she put the blame squarely on God. Naomi acted as if she had no understanding of the goodness and mercy of God. Instead of being bitter at the loss of her family, she should have been counting her blessings (though they may have appeared to be few in her eyes). In Ruth 1:20, Naomi declares, "Do not call me Naomi (*Delight, Pleasant One*), call me Mara (*Bitter*) for God has

dealt very bitterly with me. I went out *full (the greatest possible, maximum)*, and the Lord has brought me home again *empty (destitute, devoid).*" Was Ruth not considered to be a part of Naomi's family? Naomi acted as if she did not consider Ruth as part of her *full* family since she used the word *empty* to define her current situation (of course, that was the bitterness talking). However, Naomi continually called Ruth her daughter. Grief can become an overwhelming part of our lives if we do not allow the Word of God to bring us back to a place where we acknowledge His goodness and mercy.

We often find ourselves in almost the same frame of mind and heart (sometimes the same) as Naomi. Bitterness will take root (Hebrews 12:15) if we allow it. When we start looking at God as the enemy and blaming our misfortunes on Him, bitterness will quickly begin to control our lives. Even though we may not see bitterness in a person with our naked eyes, bitterness will manifest in several ways.

Bitterness is a root; therefore, like plant roots, it will grow and fester below the surface. God warned us to avoid bitterness, characterized by negativity, critical attitudes,

resentfulness, and an unforgiving spirit. Even though the Bible does not record it, I imagine there were days, especially after losing her husband and two sons, that Naomi was not very nice to Ruth or maybe even resented her. When we are bitter, we want everyone around us to be bitter as well. Ephesians 4:31-32 admonishes us to eliminate all bitterness and practice what God taught us about love and forgiveness.

To remove this poisonousness root from our lives, we need to practice forgiveness. If we are bitter due to what others have done (or what we perceived they have done), we need to start with forgiveness. I believe Naomi held deep anger toward her husband as well as towards God. She was angry at Elimelech because he took her to Moab, where she was left empty, and she blamed God for allowing this to happen. Unforgiveness, like bitterness, is a poison. It can cause emotional and physical problems. We start to maintain a grotesque image of ourselves and others. Naomi held a distorted image of herself. She saw herself as empty; God saw her as *full*; she saw herself as broken and damaged; God saw perfection. We need to learn to see

ourselves as God sees us. We are to be transformed into His glorious image from glory to glory (2 Corinthians 3:18).

Ruth was not bitter at her loss; she was determined to be a blessing to her mother-in-law even though her loss was as significant as Naomi's (Ruth 1:16-17). Ruth was the catalyst that started to melt Naomi's stony heart. As the seasons passed and Naomi's circumstances began to improve, the root of bitterness in her heart began to dissolve. I believe her mother/daughter relationship with Ruth helped heal the broken places in her heart. Thankfully, in the end, Naomi once again felt that her life was *full*.

Ruth, through her obedience, gained a husband and a place in the genealogy of Jesus. Ruth had no knowledge that her son would be the grandfather of King David (Ruth 4:16-22) and, therefore, in the lineage of Jesus Christ. Sometimes from significant loss comes great rewards. You may be going through a time of great sorrow and bitterness and wondering how to overcome it.

In 1 Samuel 30:6, David describes how his men grieved bitterly over their loss. Their families had been taken captive. They were talking of stoning David. Did

they somehow forget that David also had family members taken? Did they not see how he was also weeping and greatly distressed in spirit? However, David took a different approach; he strengthened (encouraged) himself by trusting God.

How can you encourage yourself in the Lord? Let's take a page out of King David's playbook. David felt he had to take the fight to the enemy, but he did not want to make a move without first hearing from God:

1. He sent for the Ephod (Priestly garment) – 1 Samuel 30:7

2. He prayed and sought permission to move– 1 Samuel 30:8

3. He closely followed God's instruction – 1 Samuel 30: 9

Why was the ephod so important? According to the *Holman Bible Dictionary*, the *Ephod (ee' fahd)* was a priestly garment connected with seeking a word from God. The Old Testament references the *ephod* as a relatively simple, linen garment, possibly a short skirt, apron, or loincloth. 1 Samuel 14:3 and 1 Samuel 22:18 identified the *ephod* as a priestly garment worn by Samuel (Samuel 2:18).

David wore an *ephod* when he danced before God when the Ark of the Covenant was transferred to the capital city of Jerusalem (2 Samuel 6:14). The *ephod* was associated with the presence of God or of those who had a special relationship with God. As a source of divine guidance, David used the *ephod* to determine if he could trust the people of Kelilah (1 Samuel 23:9-12). As previously noted, David called for the *ephod* to decide whether he should pursue the Amalekites (1 Samuel 30:7-8).

David took the time to have a conversation with God. **He prayed**. Why take time to pray when the time was of great essence? From Genesis through Revelations, God instructs us to pray. Prayer is our lifeline; it keeps us connected to the source. The first prayer in the Bible (Genesis 3:8-13) is a conversation initiated by God, speaking with Adam and Eve after they had sinned. Pay attention here; if we know we have sinned, God knows we have sinned, but He still longs to have a conversation with us. Philippians 4:6 admonishes us to "be anxious for nothing, … in everything by prayer and supplication with thanksgiving let your requests be made known to God." The Word directs us to "pray without ceasing" (1

Thessalonians 5:17). David knew God, and He knew that God had the answers needed in this situation. After praying, David followed God's instructions.

When we pray and ask God to help us with a particular situation, we need to follow His instructions. God will not move or advance you beyond your last act of disobedience. Do you continually find yourself in the same *mess* time after time? Check your obedience. Are you obeying God's instructions, or are you playing by your own rules? David knew that he had to follow God's instructions if he wanted to get his family back.

In the end, David recovered all that was taken, with no loss of life. This life lesson reminds us that bitterness is a satanic trap; however, calling on God and following His instructions leads you out of the schemes set up by your enemies into victory.

Desire a Good Reputation

Proverbs 22:1 urges us to choose a good reputation over great riches. Furthermore, being held in high esteem is better than silver or gold. Ruth considered her reputation when she moved to Bethlehem with Naomi. She could have gone *a-whoring* (committing sexual sins) after many rich young men in Bethlehem to get a husband or make a few dollars. Ruth did not want to bring dishonor to Naomi or Naomi's family. Remember, she had decided to honor Naomi's God as her God. Take a look at Ruth's ancestral history.

According to a *Midrash* legend, Ruth was a princess from Moab, daughter of King Eglon. The text indicates that Eglon had two daughters named Orpah and Ruth, making Ruth and Orpah sisters and sisters-in-law. Ruth was born into and raised in a culture where they worshipped *Chemosh*, the destroyer, subduer, or fish god. Followers of *Chemosh* engaged in sorcery, adultery, incest, prostitution, and the sacrifice of unwanted children in the fire (infanticide). Ruth was not the only woman of questionable lineage or character to make her way into the Biblical

record. Rahab, a prostitute from Jericho (Joshua 2), made the list (Matthew 1:5), along with Tamar (Matthew 1:3), who entered the royal bloodline by disguising herself as a harlot and seducing Judah to impregnate her (because of the unjust way he treated her (Genesis 38). Mary, Jesus' mother, is included in the list. She became pregnant with Jesus outside of marriage and claimed a miraculous conception (Matthew 1:16).

God chose to intertwine His glorious grace throughout the Bible. God is a redemptive God, and He takes pleasure in redeeming sinners from every corner of the globe. Ruth accepted redemption when she decided to leave Moab with Naomi. She put aside all those pagan rituals she had learned in Moab and decided to pursue life as a child of the true King (not King Eglon, her earthly father). When Boaz met Ruth, he declared,

> "I've been told all about what you have done for your mother-in-law since the death of your husband—how you left your father and mother and your homeland and came to live with a people you did not know before. May the Lord repay you for what you have done. May you be richly rewarded

by the Lord, the God of Israel, under whose wings you have come to take refuge" (Ruth 2:11-12). He further declares in Ruth 3:11, "Now don't worry about a thing, my daughter. I will do what is necessary, for everyone in town knows you are a virtuous woman."

John Gill's Commentary on the Book of Ruth tells us more about Ruth's virtue stating,

> "..or righteous, as the Targum; a good woman, possessed of grace and virtue, having every agreeable qualification to recommend to the marriage state; and therefore, should they come to the knowledge of the step taken to obtain it, will never reproach thee for it, nor blame me for marrying a person, though poor, of such an excellent character, which, by her conduct and behavior, was universally established" (Gill, 1763, para. 3).

What would the town's people have to say about you? Would you be considered a virtuous woman? Ruth chose virtue over everything else. She was new to Bethlehem and already had a reputation that revealed her character and faith, despite her lineage. Maintaining purity is the life

lesson in this chapter. In Colossians 3:5, Paul admonishes us,

> "So put to death and deprive of power the evil longings of your earthly body [with its sensual, self-centered instincts] immorality, impurity, sinful passion, evil desire, and greed, which is [a kind of] idolatry [because it replaces your devotion to God]."

Display Humility in the Midst of Conflict

Ruth remained humble during all that she went through. Starting with the death of her husband, Mahlon, and continuing through her journey to Bethlehem, and finally securing a place for herself and Naomi after her marriage to Boaz. Author and radio host Nancy Leigh Demoss said, "Gratitude is the overflow of a humble heart, just as surely as an ungrateful, complaining spirit flows out of a proud heart." James 4:10 counsels us to "humble yourselves [feeling very insignificant] in the presence of the Lord, and He will exalt you [He will lift you up and make your lives significant]." Ruth was the very picture of humility. She did not insist on having her way nor make demands of others so she could gain favor.

Ruth put aside all of herself to allow Naomi to prosper. Did it ever occur to you that Ruth may not have been looking for a husband to bring happiness into her life? The spirit of humility that abounds in Ruth was how she humbly allowed her feelings to be overshadowed by her concern and gratitude to Naomi.

Ruth 1:14 illustrates Ruth's love for Naomi. Orpah left and returned to her people, but Ruth *cleaved* to Naomi. *Cleaved (dâbaq)* means to stick to, adhere to, join with, stay with, and stay in close proximity. This word is the same as the noun form for "*glue.*" The first use of *dâbaq* is in Genesis 2:24 and speaks of the union of man and woman. The word is also used to convey the relationship we should have with God (Deuteronomy 11:22). In other words, Ruth stuck to Naomi like glue, and we should stick to God in the same manner. It is this type of relationship, which causes us to walk in humility before God.

Let's follow Jesus as our ultimate example of humility. He was obedient to the Father by humbling Himself all of the way to a violent death on the cross.

After He was found in [terms of His] outward appearance as a man [for a divinely-appointed time], He humbled Himself [still further] by becoming obedient [to the Father] to the point of death, even death on a cross. For this reason also [because He obeyed and so completely humbled Himself], God has highly exalted Him and bestowed on Him the name which is above every

name, so that at the name of Jesus every knee shall bow [in submission], of those who are in heaven and on earth and under the earth, and that every tongue will confess *and* openly acknowledge that Jesus Christ is Lord (sovereign God), to the glory of God the Father (Philippians 2:8-11).

Because Jesus chose to go the cross, God exalted Him just like how it says He will exalt us. Trust God, He will do all He has promised.

Therefore humble yourselves under the mighty hand of God [set aside self-righteous pride], so that He may exalt you [to a place of honor in His service] at the appropriate time, casting all your cares [all your anxieties, all your worries, and all your concerns, once and for all] on Him, for He cares about you [with deepest affection, and watches over you very carefully] (1 Peter 5:6-7).

We see Ruth following this notion time after time. She goes out to the fields to work (Ruth 2:3), worked through the barley harvest and the wheat harvest, from March through June (Ruth 2:23), she heeded the advice of her mother-in-law (Ruth 3:5), she humbled herself before

Boaz (Ruth 2:10, 13), and she did not go after rich men (Ruth 3:10).

Ruth did not display false flattery; she showed the expressions of a heart operating out of humble gratitude. The life lesson is to remain humble and grateful for all God has given you. Remember being grateful is the result of a life lived with humility.

Talking Shoes

Years ago, there was a television show called *Boston Public*. It was a story about a public high school, *Winslow*, in Boston. One of the characters in the show was a bus driver named Mrs. Parks. Mrs. Parks frequently stopped by the school to file a complaint and tell everyone, especially the principal, to **smell that shoe**. She wanted everyone to understand that *shoes can and do talk*. They often tell a story. For Mrs. Parks, the story was I *have something to say, and you better stop and listen to what I have to say*. Even though what she had to say did not make a lot of sense to anyone except herself.

In Ruth 4:7-8, the *talking shoe* tells a story of Boaz and *the redeemer* coming to an agreement which meant Boaz had bought everything that was previously Elimelech's and everything that was Chilion's and Mahlon's from the hand of Naomi. He also acquired Ruth, the widow of Mahlon, to be his wife to restore the name of the deceased to his inheritance. This agreement also meant that the name of the dead *would not be cut off* from his brothers or the gate of his birthplace (Ruth 4:9, 10). In the

Old Testament, "feet" and "shoes" symbolized power, possession, and domination (Joshua 10:24, Psalm 8:6, 60:8, 108:9).

Feet and shoes also played symbolic roles in ancient property transactions. The *Nuzi Texts*, tablets found in an ancient city of Nuzi in N.E. Iraq, tell of practices similar to those in Genesis, such as adoption for childless couples (Genesis 15:2), children by proxy (Genesis 16; 21:1), inheritance rights (Genesis 25:29), and levirate marriage (Genesis 38; Deuteronomy 25:5). In the Old Testament, to "set foot" on the land was associated with ownership of it (Deuteronomy 1:36, 11:24; Joshua 1:3, 14:9); thus, the sandal transfer in Ruth 4:7 (*talking shoe*) could be a symbolic gesture of such ancient customs.

In the New Testament, Paul's view of sandals/shoes is a positive one. Paul in writing to the church in Ephesus in c.60-62 AD used a formidable image of how we as Christians should adorn ourselves when we go forth into the world for Christian service. Starting in Ephesians 6:10, Paul encourages us to "be strong in the Lord [draw your strength from Him and be empowered through your union with Him] and in the power of His [boundless] might". In

Ephesians 6:15, Paul admonishes us to "shod our feet" or "having strapped on your feet the gospel of peace in preparation [to face the enemy with firm-footed stability and the readiness produced by the good news]".

The sandals worn by Romans soldiers were made from leather, lace around the ankle, and fastened part way up the calf. However, these sandals were different from what the average person wore in the marketplace. The sandals were fitted with spikes on the bottom of the sole. The soldiers had to battle in all kinds of terrain, in all kinds of weather, and at all hours of the day. The spikes helped them maintain their footing. The spikes allowed them to, as Paul repeats four times in Ephesians 6:10-14, 'to stand firm in the battle'.

Ephesians 6 gives us a picture of a soldier getting ready for battle. Paul is showing us how to adorn ourselves each day to do battle against the forces of our enemy.

> "Put on the full armor of God [for His precepts are like the splendid armor of a heavily-armed soldier], so that you may be able to [successfully] stand up against all the schemes *and* the strategies *and* the deceits of the devil. For our struggle is not against

flesh and blood [contending only with physical opponents], but against the rulers, against the powers, against the world forces of this [present] darkness, against the spiritual *forces* of wickedness in the heavenly (supernatural) *places*. Therefore, put on the complete armor of God, so that you will be able to [successfully] resist *and* stand your ground in the evil day [of danger], and having done everything [that the crisis demands], to stand firm [in your place, fully prepared, immovable, victorious]. So, stand firm *and* hold your ground, having tightened the wide band of truth (personal integrity, moral courage) around your waist and having put on the breastplate of righteousness (an upright heart), and having strapped on your feet the gospel of peace in preparation [to face the enemy with firm-footed stability and the readiness produced by the good news]. Above all, lift up the [protective] shield of faith with which you can extinguish all the flaming arrows of the evil *one*. And take the helmet of salvation, and the sword of the Spirit, which is the

Word of God. With all prayer and petition pray [with specific requests] at all times [on every occasion and in every season] in the Spirit, and with this in view, stay alert with all perseverance and petition [interceding in prayer] for all God's people (Ephesians 6:10-18).

The lesson of the *talking shoe* is that we are constantly making agreements with others. These agreements (covenants) are important to God. He made covenants with Abraham, Moses, David, and a new covenant with us through Jesus Christ. He swore on no one other than Himself that He would always keep His covenants. We discover throughout scripture that God is a covenant-keeping God, and the *talking shoe* is His Word.

Can I Get a Goel?

A *Goel* is a person who ransoms or redeems someone. This term is found 18 times in the Old Testament (13 times in Isaiah alone). It describes a close relative, a *kinsman-redeemer*, who assumes the role of *ge'ulla*— *"redemption or recovery"* for the relative. Instructions concerning the *gō'ēl* duties fall within the treatment of the Jubilee Year in Leviticus 25:8-55. God loves His people so much that He provided a *safety net* for their vulnerabilities. He showed himself to be a powerful protector of the weak.

A Kinsman Redeemer must meet these five requirements:

1. He must be a close relative [related by blood] (Leviticus 25:48; 25:25 Ruth 3:12, 13).

2. He must have the ability to redeem. (Ruth 4:6). He must be free of any disaster or need for redemption.

3. He must be willing to redeem. He might be willing conceivably and yet not have the ability to redeem the individual concerned (Ruth 4:6).

4. Redemption was completed when the price was paid entirely (Leviticus 25:27; Ruth 4:7-11).

5. He was required to redeem. If he failed to redeem for any reason, he was humiliated (Ruth 4).

The duties of the *goel* included buying back or redeeming someone sold into slavery (Leviticus 25:47-49), buying back property sold due to poverty (Leviticus 25:25-27), marrying the childless widow of his kin (Deuteronomy 25:5, Ruth 3:13), and avenging the blood of a near relative (Numbers 35: 9-34).

Why do we need a redeemer? God gave Adam and Eve dominion over the earth. In Genesis 1:28, God blessed them and said to them, be fruitful and multiply, and fill the earth. Subdue it and rule over every living thing that moves on the earth. In Genesis 3, Eve listened to the lies of the enemy, Satan. She was deceived and also led Adam to sin; in other words, they believed **THE LIE**. They ate of the tree of the knowledge of good and evil and relinquished their ownership of what God had given them.

So, God kicked Adam out; and at the east of the garden of Eden, He stationed the cherubim and the flaming sword which turned every direction to guard the way to the

tree of life. God made sure that man did not have access to the tree, demolished man's ability to eat and live forever as a sinner (Genesis 3:24). God had a plan.

Romans 5:12 states, "Therefore, just as sin came into the world through one man, and death through sin, so death spread to all people [no one being able to stop it or escape its power] because they all sinned." God planned for our redemption through our Goel. Our Lord Jesus Christ is our true *Goel*. He has spiritually fulfilled all required tasks. He is our deliverer (redeemer) out of the devil's bondage (Hebrews 2:15); He gave us life everlasting (John 1:4; John 1:12-13); He is the redeemer of our inheritance (Ephesians 1:11-14), and He shall execute judgment as the "slayer" of God, the just judge (John 5:27).

This lesson is to remember that we are not alone in the world. God loves us and has a plan for our redemption. He never intended for us to stay lost and under the control of the evil one. When Jesus died on the cross, he said, 'It is finished' (John 19:28-30). Our debts have been canceled. When you were dead in your sins and in the uncircumcision of your flesh (worldliness, manner of life), God made you alive together with Christ, having [freely] forgiven us all

our sins, having canceled out the certificate of debt consisting of legal demands [which were in force] against us and which were hostile to us. And this certificate He has set aside *and* completely removed by nailing it to the cross (Colossians 2:13-14). Thank God for our *Goel*.

Fulfilling Your Divine Purpose

Ruth 4:13 – "So Boaz took Ruth, and she became his wife.
And he went into her, and the Lord enabled her to
conceive, and she gave birth to a son".

Boaz is not mentioned again after this verse. He
disappears. According to *Yalkut Shimoni 608,* a midrash of
Biblical passages arranged according to portions of the
Hebrew Bible, Boaz died that very night having fulfilled
the purpose of God by obeying God in marrying Ruth and
giving her a son. When we follow our agenda, not God's,
we pursue delusions; only God knows our true purpose.
Boaz spent many years as a leader in Israel. However, he
did not realize that his divine purpose was to wait for a
widowed, Moabite woman to wander into his grain field
and his field of vision. Marrying her and producing the
seed of the Messiah was his life's purpose in this world,
and afterward, his natural life came to an end. Ruth also
had a purpose to fulfill. The blessing of the townspeople in
Ruth 4:11-12 is spoken over Ruth,

> "May the Lord make this woman who is coming
> into your home like Rachel and Leah, from whom
> all the nation of Israel descended! May you prosper

in Ephrathah and be famous in Bethlehem. And
may the Lord give you descendants by this young
woman who will be like those of our ancestor Perez,
the son of Tamar and Judah".

The fulfillment of this blessing is a joyous offspring named
Obed (*worshipper*), who was the father of Jesse and King
David's grandfather and is named in the genealogy of
Jesus.

The references to Rachel, Leah, and Tamar in the
blessing function as a way not only to welcome Ruth into
the community by linking her with the mothers of that
community but also lead us to perceive Ruth in the role of
the heroic woman who ensured the preservation of the
people of Israel. Ruth has the distinction of being the only
woman in the Bible to be unequivocally called an *eshet
hayil* (a woman of valor). The term *hayil* typically applies
to men. While she struggled mightily to preserve Mahlon's
name, she has immortalized her name, winning the hearts
of readers generation after generation. The story of Ruth
establishes a pattern of redemption and perpetuation of the
family for David. The patriarchal line is continued through
the deeds of women—and it thereby joins the covenant

with David to the covenant with Abraham.

The book of Ruth paints a picture of faith, loyalty, love, and family. In many ways, Ruth and Naomi's lives are no different from ours. We desire a good reputation, a nice place to live, provisions, the blessings and respect of our neighbors, and the love of family. I pray these lessons inspired you to look at yourself in the mirror of God's mercy and grace and choose to follow the plans and purposes He has ordained for you. We are part of that family. Galatians 3:29 tells us, "…if you belong to Christ [if you are in Him], then you are Abraham's descendants, and [spiritual] heirs according to [God's] promise."

Books by Garnet Nowell

Hey, Don't Be That Girl 21-Day Devotional

Hey, Don't Be That Girl Devotional Journal

Praying Through the Pandemic:
Ignite Your Faith, Conquer Your Fear

Being: Manifesting the Image of God

Want more inspiration? Visit my blog:
Inspiration Flows @
www.inspirationflows.com

Follow me on Facebook, LinkedIn